Priscilla
from where
the Pine Trees
Whisper

THE ADVENTURES OF A YOUNG CHILD

Marian Miller Stutzman

PRISCILLA FROM WHERE THE PINE TREES WHISPER

THE ADVENTURES OF A YOUNG CHILD

Marian Miller Stutzman

ISBN: 978-1-4834-3979-2 (sc)
ISBN: 978-1-4834-3978-5 (e)

Because of the dynamic nature of the Internet, any web addresses or links contained in
this book may have changed since publication and may no longer be valid. The views
expressed in this work are solely those of the author and do not necessarily reflect the
views of the publisher, and the publisher hereby disclaims any responsibility for them.

Any people depicted in stock imagery provided by Thinkstock are models,
and such images are being used for illustrative purposes only.
Certain stock imagery © Thinkstock.

Lulu Publishing Services rev. date: 12/09/2015

She woke up and jumped out of bed anxious to start a new day. She looked in her dresser mirror and hurriedly grabbed a comb and put a few good strokes in her hair. It was a beautiful summer day of June in 1950 in South Carolina and she was a happy girl who loved summer and the outdoors. Her parents and her lived in a small cottage home near a river. Big tall pine trees surrounded their house. She was nine years old and the oldest in a family of four. Their house was made of simple slabs of wood that were put together to make a cozy simple home. In her bedroom two of her younger sisters had a bed in there too where they slept in together since they were so small yet. Her brother slept in a room across the hall. He was their only brother and the youngest of them all. They did not have running water so they had to walk a quarter mile every day with a pail and get their drinking water from a spring where the water came from underground. Since she was the oldest, that job was hers every day. Her younger sisters would sometimes go along and help by bringing a small pail. It was very good drinking water but they had to be careful how much they used or they would have to make another trip before evening came. They would get water to wash their clothes from the river that was about 20 feet away. Between their house and the storage shed they had was a big black kettle and it was hung on 2 strong posts with a board that went across and the kettle had a chain on each side to hold it up to the structure. Beside that they had an old wringer washer that was mounted on a platform of boards nailed together and 4 posts which consisted of a post at each corner to hold up the tin that the roof was made of. Since they had so many pine trees around their house they would gather broken tree limbs and twigs to start a fire to heat up water in the kettle to do their laundry. Then they would hang the laundry on the lines they had strung from tree to tree. Their garden was near the house and they always had plenty of vegetables during the summer, and in mid summer and fall they would can everything they could so they had plenty to eat in the winter too. She loved summer days like these and she had so much she wanted to do but of course she had to hoe the garden in the hot sun too or else the weeds would take over. Her mother often called her name because she was the oldest and her younger sisters were still too young to get much accomplished. One thing they loved to do was go on a walk in the forest to explore the woods and watch nature. Sometimes on a walk with her younger sisters and brother trailing behind she would tell them to be quiet and they would sneak up close enough to see a baby fawn hiding in some high grass. But today she was excited because she had made a make shift raft and she wanted to try it in the river. She knew her mother would probably not approve but being young like she was her exploring instincts to try new things sometimes took over. She had nailed together a couple boards of slab boards laying around and underneath she had fastened a couple of empty plastic barrels that were laying around and tied them on by looping twine through the handles and then tied them tightly to the raft. She knew it would float because she had put it in the water yesterday and watched it float down the river attached to the twine that she had tied to it still in her hand so she could control where it went. But she did not have time yesterday to see if it supported her weight and if she could use it to row down the river with the two 4 foot boards she had for paddles. It seemed to her like everytime she was doing something really fun she would hear her mother call her name to help or do something. She knew if she heard her mom call that she had better run or she would get in trouble, because work always came first in this family. After she had brushed her hair and slipped on her clothes, she made her bed and went down the ladder that they used to go upstairs to their bedrooms. Her mom was putting wood in the stove despite the warm tempature outside. The stove needed to be hot so they could cook their breakfast on it. She quickly set the table without being told as that was her daily chore, and then headed outdoors with an empty egg carton to gather eggs from their chicken house that they had outback near their small two story barn. The two red roosters they had were not very friendly so she was always careful and not get too near to them, and to carry a small stick just in case they decided to chase her. The chickens were usually out of the chicken house as soon as it was daylight but sometimes a chicken decided to stay longer on her eggs and she had to chase them off. The chickens did not like to be chased off of their nest of eggs and would squawk and protest loudly and run out of the chicken house telling every other chicken how someone was stealing their eggs. One of the red roosters would usually come over and think this was a good time to show off his charm to the upset chicken. She hurried into the chicken house and to her delight no chickens were in sight. She gathered all the eggs and took them in the house and gave them to her mother. Her mother cracked a few and put some in a cast iron skillet that was already on the stove that was hot and ready. They raised their own corn in the large fields they had beside the river so they usually had corn meal mush for breakfast with eggs. They had one cow that was a jersey and she gave rich milk. She was very tame and her dad usually milked her before he went to work. Her dad worked in an underground mine. After the cow was milked whatever was not used for breakfast was put in the spring which was always cool so the milk would stay cool and keep longer. That was usually one of her younger sisters job to take the milk down to the spring, as she had to wash the dishes and put them away. Today she was excited about trying out her new raft that she had put together yesterday, so she happily pitched in and helped her mother get breakfast ready. After her father came in from milking the cow, she strained the milk to make sure their was no dirt in it and set a pitcher of milk on the table. Everything was ready to eat and on the table so they all sat down and bowed their heads and said grace. Everyone seemed hungry and passed around the food. Some of the younger ones had just got up so they were still rubbing their eyes. She noticed her sisters hair needed combing, so after breakfast she helped them comb and pull back their hair. Then she washed the dishes while her sisters got out a towel to dry them off and help put them away. When all the dishes were put away and the floor was swept she knew the morning chores were done and now she had some time to herself for at least an hour or so. She waited until everyone was occupied then she quietly slipped away to where her raft was tied to a tree beside the river. She untied it and cautiously waded in the river with the raft with her bare feet. She tested it by gently sitting on it first, and when she saw it supported her weight she put both feet up and before she knew it she was floating down the river quite fast. The water flowed downstream gently but if she was not careful she noticed she was much further downstream then what it seemed like if you were just watching the water. She was actually very proud of herself for making this raft and it gave her a sense of happiness to peacefully float downstream and watch the water flow and see the fish jump out of the water around her. She knew she was lucky that the water was gentle and the current was not too strong. After about a half hour she decided it was time to head back. Going back she decided was a lot more work then going downstream, because she was wading and pulling the raft and the water was tugging at it. Finally after another half hour of wading she was back to where she had started and she quickly tied the raft to a tree and started walking swiftly towards the house to make sure nobody was looking for her. She felt happy about her experiment but she knew if her parents knew what she had been doing they would have been worried. When she arrived at the house her younger sisters were pushing each other on a make shift swing that they had made. They had used their dads baler twine and climbed up the big tree they had outside the house and tied the ends to the limb. Her mom was inside sewing and mending clothes that she took in from people to help make ends meet. Her mom was always busy so a lot of the time she did not have time to always make sure her children were not climbing trees or other stuff. Priscilla was the oldest and did her best to look after her younger siblings too, but sometimes she needed to get away a little too. She saw her sisters were having fun and were occupied, so she headed in the house. She saw it was getting close to lunch time so she got a pail and headed out to their underground root cellar to get some potatoes that they had stored there from last fall. She always dreaded opening the door because inside it smelled musky and it was dark and the door had cobwebs. Sometimes she was afraid that she would find a snake in there. But so far she never did. She opened the door and looked inside and it looked ok so she grabbed some potatoes threw them in her bucket and ran out. She went in the house and put them in a stainless steel bowl and started peeling them to get them ready to have mashed potatoes for lunch. After they were peeled she cut them up and put them in a pot on the stove and put water in it to cook until they got soft. Then she went outside to play with her sisters and see what they were doing.

They had quit swinging and were now playing in the sandbox they had outside near the house with boards put together in a square box made of lumber to keep the sand in. Her sisters were making a sand castle and trying to see who could make the biggest one. She decided she was going to join in and help them. She almost forgot about her potatoes on the stove after getting in on the action. She told her sisters she had to go check on making lunch and that they should come in the house in fifteen minutes to set the table. When she came in the house the potatoes were boiling vigorously so she grabbed a fork and poked them to see if they were soft. They were soft so she grabbed two potholders and lifted them off the stove and carried them to the sink where she put the lid on crooked and poured the water out. It was important to get all the water out before she mashed them, because if she did not get all the water out the potatoes would turn lumpy. After she had carefully dumped all the water out she got out a potatoe masher in the drawer and started mashing them. The steam from dumping out the water made her forehead feel hot and sweaty. Her mom was taking a break from sewing and was now rocking her younger brother and reading a book to him. After she was almost certain the potatoes were mashed without a lump, she sprinkled salt in them and then added a big scoop of homemade butter that they made from the cream from their cows milk. To make the butter they would let the milk stand for at least a half hour and then take a dipper and dip off the cream that gathered on the top. Then they would put the cream in a quart jar and usually it was one of her younger sisters job to shake it until it turned to butter. After she had added the salt and butter to her potatoes she got the milk left over from breakfast that was in a pitcher on the countertop and poured about half a cup of milk in the potatoes and whipped it in by using the potatoe masher and going around in the pot in swift circular motions. It was not the right texture yet so she kept adding small amounts of milk until it was just right. She got a big spoon and scooped out the mashed potatoes and put the them in a bowl and covered it and put it on the table. By now her sisters had come in, so they started setting the table because they were hungry and could not wait to eat. She had to make gravy too and a vegetable so she ran down to their cellar and got a can of canned venison and a can of corn where they kept all their canned foods on the shelves that her dad had made. She had put over a pan of water before she went to the cellar so by the time she came back it was boiling. She got out some flour and put it in a small bowl and added some spices and whipped it with some water so it had no clumps of flour. Now she opened the jar of venison and put half of it in the pan she had hot water in for the gravy. Next she waited until the meat was hot then she added the mixture of flour she had in a bowl and stirred it quickly until it got thick and then she poured it into a small dish and put it on the table. Her mom had put the corn on the stove to heat and sliced some homemade bread to go with the butter and applebutter and the fresh tomatoes they had from the garden. Dad was at work so it was just them today. Her mom had packed her dad a lunch to eat at work. It was quite warm out so after eating they all went to their bedroom to read or take a nap before they did the dishes. She decided to read a book she had that one of her friends had loaned her to read. She loved to read but did not always have time to read as much as she wanted to. She laid on her back in the bed in her room and holding the book above her she began to read about a exciting adventure. She almost forgot where she was until she heard her mom calling her name to do the dishes. After everyone had helped put away all the dishes. She and her sisters went out to hoe and pull weeds in the garden. They were almost done when they saw a big hawk hovering over one of their chickens. Priscilla knew what that meant so she ran as fast as she could and tried to yell and scream to scare him, but the hawk did not seem to scare easy and was determined to get his prey. By then the hawk had ahold of the chicken and despite her doing all she could he flew off with it. The sight of seeing him flying away with one of their smaller chickens made her stomach sick. She went inside to tell her mom. Her mom said from now on they had to try and keep the chickens more in the trees near the house so a hawk can't see them as well. They usually let the chickens wander around their house freely to eat the grasshoppers and bugs etc. The road that went past their house was a dirt road so their were very few cars that went past a day, and the chickens were tame and liked their freedom. With them not penned up all the time and since they ate bugs and grass their yolks of the egg were much richer and deeper yellow. When they had bread that was getting moldy they would stand on the front porch and coax them to come near and throw pieces out to them.It was funny how they would watch you throw a piece and then run for it. Priscilla liked to throw out a big chunk of bread and then watch a chicken trying to gulp it down. It looked like the chicken was so desperate

tired to sit down at the table so they could eat and talk about their day. Her dad went over to wash up in a basin of water. After he was all washed up he went over and sat down at the table. The rest of the family had sat down too because they were all hungry. The stew was delicious and there was fresh homemade bread to go with it. Priscilla could not wait to have the dishes done and put away, and to relax for the evening. After the evening dishes were done and the house was swept she would be free for the evening until bedtime. As soon as everyone was done she got up and started clearing up the table and taking the dishes to the sink to wash them. When all was washed and put away she went to her room and lighted her little kerosene lamp that was on her night stand beside her bed. Then she got her book she had been reading and flopped down on the bed and breathed a sigh of relief. She loved evenings like these to read and think about things and ideas that she wanted to check out. Soon she got lost in her book and was in another world. Her sisters were outside playing and she could hear them from her room. They liked being outside and would usually play until dusk. Her younger brother was playing beside her dad who was sitting on his easy chair reading the newspaper. Her mom was sitting on the couch mending something with a thread and needle in her hands. From where she was in her room upstairs she could look downstairs through the hole where their wooden ladder came through that they used to go up and down the stairs. Their room was simple but neat and comfortable. Priscilla had a night stand by her bed with a kerosene lamp on it. On the other side of the room her sisters each had a small night stand with a kerosene oil lamp on their side of their bed. They did not have any extra luxuries but just what they needed to have in order to live a normal happy life. Their blankets were a simple quilt her mom had pieced together from material that her mother had salvaged from scraps of material that were left over from clothes that were no longer able to be worn. All their clothing that they wore was sewed by her mom. After the clock chimed nine she knew it was time to close her book and get ready for bed. Her sisters were already inside and washing their bare feet in a basin of water. She waited until they were done then she helped her sisters and brother go upstairs on the ladder. They all said their prayers then got ready for bed. Priscilla tucked her brother in bed and gave him a kiss on the forehead and then went to her own room. Her brother had his own bedroom across the hall but the door was always open so he did not feel alone. Her sisters crawled in their bed just two feet across from hers. Her sisters proceeded to tell Priscilla about what they did today, and then Loretta and Emma started giggling and teased each other for a bit. They were all tired from a long day and after about 10 minutes she heard her sisters snoring and that was the last she remembered before she drifted off to sleep. She barely even knew she was asleep before she heard her mothers voice calling for them to get up. She rolled over and yawned then slowly got out of bed. She looked out the window and saw it was going to be another beautiful sunny South Carolina summer day. She loved these days. They could do a lot of fun things in the summer. The summers in South Carolina were for the major part relaxed. When school started it would get a little different. But summers certainly was the time for them to play outside and explore the woods. Priscilla got dressed and combed her hair then went over and climbed down the ladder. Her younger sisters usually slept a little later. Her mom was making pancakes which was a treat. She noticed the pine trees branches were slightly waving outside the open window in the wind. That she assumed meant that it was nice and breezy outside. She picked up a small pail then went outside to gather the eggs. When she got near the chicken house she saw a huge black garden snake sliding after a hen and her new chicks. She knew what the snake was up to, so she quickly ran and got the biggest stick she could find. Then she approached the snake who was eyeing the small chicks. Just when the snake was almost near enough to grab a small chick Priscilla hit it on the head with her stick. The snake did not even act like she hit it because it was that determined to get the meal it had in it's mind. She used all the strength she had and hit it again. This time it felt the pain and curled up and changed it's mind and slithered away. She really wanted that snake dead but she did not have a rock or hoe near her and by the time she looked around for a rock the snake was gone. The situation made her hair stand up on her neck and arms. But she knew for now she had done the best she can.

She finished gathering the eggs then she went inside to help her mom set the table. As she was setting the table she told her mom what had happened. Her mom told her that it was very brave of her to do that but she had to always be careful. Her sisters were coming down the ladder that worked as a stairs and were still rubbing their eyes. Priscilla told her sisters to wash their hands and faces and prepared a basin full of water for them. Her brother had to have help to go up and down the stairs so she told Loretta to go wake him and help him down the stairs. Since the stairs were made like a ladder they had to be careful. It did not take Loretta long to come downstairs with her brother Joseph in tow. Her brother looked like he was ready for the day because as soon his feet touched the floor he was already laughing and running around the table. Her brother was very active and always on his feet. Her dad came in with their cows morning milking. Priscillia got the pail from him and strained the milk through a thin piece of cloth and poured it in its jug. They had nice cold milk from last nights milking that had been brought from the spring where they kept it to preserve it and keep it nice and cool. She put the fresh milk aside to be taken to the spring after breakfast. Her mom put the pancakes on the table and they all sat down to eat. Her brother sat in his highchair and seemed to really enjoy the pancakes and she laughed at how his face was all sticky with maple syrup. After they were done her dad headed off to work with the lunch mom had packed him for his day of work at the mine. She watched him drive their noisy car out the driveway then she went to take care of all the dirty dishes. Washing dishes three times a day seemed to be a chore to her sometimes, but she found out the sooner she got to it, the sooner she had time to do what she wanted.

What Priscillia was excited about today was she wanted to go exploring in the woods and try to find some golden seal. She had heard people could get quite a bit of money for golden seal by digging it up and drying it and selling it to a herb guy in town that would come out and personally look at herbs people had to sell. In her head she could envision what she would do with the money. When she went with her mother or father to town about once every 2 months she would look at the nice stuff the store had on the shelves and think about how she would one day buy what she wanted. She really liked the flowered frilly ruffled dresses. Her dresses were more plain and worn. Her only two good dresses were used only for very special occasions. After the dishes were done and the floor was swept she asked her mom if she could go for a walk in the woods. Her mom said yes but to not go to far and to always be careful. Priscilla assured her that she would, and that she would be back in about an hour or so. She told her mom about her plan to try to find some golden seal and she had heard it grows in the woods and that it was worth quite a bit of money. Her mom said that she thought it sounded like a good idea and wished her good luck on finding some. Priscilla was happy about the idea and headed out. She started out skipping along the the trail and whistling as happy as could be and just enjoying the view and beauty of nature. The further she got in the woods the more dense the woods were. About a half mile into the woods she started walking slower and looking for the description of the plant that one of her friends had described to her. One of her friends had told her it was a green plant with a red little object that was usually on top of the plant. She really hoped she could find one. She found a lot of flowers and vines and ferns but nothing that looked like what she was looking for. After about a mile into the woods she was starting to get tired and losing hope, because walking over all the logs and leaves and rocks that were in her path was not easy. She knew she had better not go to far because it was not always safe to be in the woods alone with all kinds of wild animals. Most of the animals around there were scared and hid at the slightest noise of humans but she assumed that it was better if she was always alert and on the look out. She saw a remote spot on the left in the corner of her eye by some bushes that caught her attention, so she ran over and sure enough she thought she found what she was looking for. Right in front of her was a couple of small plants that had the shape of a star and something red on it. Her heart started beating fast and her face flushed with excitement. She bent down and looked really close at the plant and was trying to think what would be the best option to dig out the roots. She knew the goldenseal root was what she wanted and not so much the plant. She saw the ground around the plants was damp and figured that a sharp stick would work to help prod and dig out the plants. She looked around for the biggest sharp stick she could find. The best one that she could see was one that was attached to a tree branch. She broke it off by twisting it and went over to her treasured patch of golden seal. She pushed the stick down as hard as she could and pushed it sideways to grip the root and try to prod it loose. She heard the groan of roots and she figured that if she kept digging aound it that it would help to make sure it all came up even and it would break loose and she would get all of the plants roots. Slowly but surely it seemed to break loose and after much careful digging she pulled out a big chunk of dirt covered roots. She brushed off the dirt with her fingers and decided to test if it was golden seal by scraping off a small part of the skin and seeing if it was a glowing yellow. Sure enough to her amazement it was indeed yellow. She picked it up and because of her excitement she was surprisingly not tired anymore. She started running and ran all the way home. She entered into the house puffing for air and yelled for her mom and sisters to come look at what she found. Her mom got up from where she was at her sewing machine and looked surprised at what Priscilla had found. Her mom patted her on the back and said she was proud of her and told her to make sure to put it on newspapers upstairs and lay it out so that it could dry properly. She grabbed some newspapers and took her golden seal root upstairs, with her sisters following her because by now they were excited and interested too. Her brother seeing and hearing the commotion was chattering and running behind them in tow. She laid out the newspaper on the floor near her window. She assumed it was best to put it where it got sunlight so it would get dry and not get moldy. She felt happy about what she had done so she picked up her brother and flopped on her bed and tickled and teased him. He squirmed and giggled with laughter. She put him back down on the floor and told him to follow her downstairs so she could help him down the ladder. Then they all went back downstairs to see if her mom needed help with something.Her mom told them it would be a good idea if they went out in the garden to pull weeds before it was time for lunch. The sun was getting warm outside so it was not exactly what she wanted to hear but she knew it had to be done. She coaxed her sisters to come with her and then they headed to the garden. When she got to the garden she noticed the weeds were indeed getting inbetween where the vegetable plants were planted. She got out a hoe from behind their shed and vigoriously started attacking the biggest weeds. She showed her sisters what were weeds and what was vegetables. With all of them together helping each other they slowly but surely got one long line of vegetables done and weed free. She stood back and looked at the work they had done. It was amazing to her the difference they had made and it made it worth the sweat that was rolling off her face and the slight backache from bending over too long. She told her sisters they were done for now and they could go play outside on their swing until lunch was ready. She winced when she saw all the little plants that Emma had pulled out thinking they were weeds. Priscilla quickly planted them all back in and covered the roots with dirt again. She sometimes wondered what was the most work doing it alone or having them help her. She assumed to herself that it was less boring this way. When she got back in the house her mom already had lunch ready. Her mom had a stack of plates on the table along with the silverware and sliced homemade bread and a jar of mayonaise to go with the freshly sliced tomatoes from their garden. They all loved tomatoes and homemade bread so this was fine with them. Their was a pitcher of chocolate milk on the table and silver cups beside it. Her mom told them they could fix themselves a plate of sandwiches and go outside to eat wherever they chose. Her mom had a extra big pile of sewing to do today, so she told them that she had already ate, but that they could go outside and eat on the lawn. Priscilla fixed her sisters and brothers a plate, then they took their plates outside and sat down on the picnic table on the lawn. Loretta decided she wanted to eat while swinging on her swing with her sandwich in her hand. Priscilla did'nt think it was the best idea, but let her do it. Joseph was sitting at the picnic table busily stuffing his face. He looked quite comical with mayonaise and tomato juice all over his face. Emma was just sitting beside Priscilla eating and swinging her feet under the table. After they were done Priscilla picked up their plates and took them inside. She quickly swooshed the dirty plates through soap and water and rinsed them, and put them on the drainer rack to dry. It was too beautiful of a day outside to stay inside, so she ran upstairs and grabbed her book and went back outside. She found a nice shady spot underneath a pine tree and sprawled down to start reading. Her sisters and brother were playing tag by now. They were laughing and chasing each other around the trees and the swing. She could hear the river's rushing water from where she was. The sound of water made her relax, and soon she was lost in her book. After awhile her eyes started getting tired so she put her book down for a minute, and before she knew it she fell asleep. She was asleep and dreaming that she was the people in her book, that she had been reading about and ready to solve a mystery, when she got awaked by one of her sisters coming over and telling her that her mom wanted her. She loved reading books about mysteries, and she also dreamed a lot about them. She got up from her comfortable spot under the big branched pine tree that had been her resting spot and picked up her book,then she headed for the house. Her mom wanted her to rock her brother because he wanted attention. She picked up her younger brother, then found a children's book and sat down on their old hickory rocker. She began rocking and telling him a story. After a couples minutes his head drooped and he was fast asleep. She quietly put the book down and gently got up and walked over to the couch and laid him on it. She picked up two pillows and put it beside him so he would not roll off. It was about three in the afternoon by now and Priscilla knew it would not be long until her dad would be coming home. He was always dirty and grimy from working, but he always had a way of cheering them up by coming home with a happy face despite his long grueling days at the mine. Her parents always seemed so happy together and they both worked hard to make their family life the best it could be. Priscilla went out to their garden and gathered some radishes, tomatoes, lettuce, sweet peppers, and onions. Her mom told her that they were having a toss salad tonite with homemade pizza. Her mom was always trying to get them to eat healthy so she tossed in vegetables wherever she could. To make pizza her mom made a simple bread dough and let it rise. After it rose she rolled it out in a pizza pan and let it rise once more. Then she would let it bake until it was done. When the dough was cooked she would take it out and pour the pizza sauce on it, and add the ingredients on top of the sauce of the pizza, which was cheese and any kind of meat. They all loved homemade bread. Her mom made it from a simple recipe of warm water with yeast to make it rise and some salt, sugar and oil. Supper was almost ready, and the smell coming from the stove was making everyone hungry. She saw her dad driving their car in the driveway with a smile on his face like usual. He was always happy at the end of a days work. Priscilla hurried and filled their water glasses on the table, and her mom set the pizza on the table on top of two pot holders. Everything was ready just as her dad walked in the door. He flung his hat on the floor and started whistling Atune, and Joseph being out doors heard it, and came running inside. Her two sisters were gathered around him asking what happened at work today. They were usually home all day so a little gossip about the town and the mine was interesting to them. Her dad was talking about some new people that had moved in town and said he heard they seemed to have quite a bit of money and that they were opening a new store in town. Her sisters asked what kind of store and if it was going to have candy in it. Her dad laughed and said it was going to be a store to sell furs, but that he assumed that their would be candy on the counter where people paid for their items that they bought. He said the husband was a trapper and set out traps every year and then skinned the animals he caught and his wife would make hats and fur coats out of them to sell. Her mom said that it sounded like fun to check out their store when it was all stocked and ready to open. Her dad said if they were good little boys and girls for their mom when he was gone at work during the day, he might take them to look at the store in town after it was open. Of course they all chorused that they would be good, because going to town shopping was a major excitement for them. Their dad would usually buy their monthly supplies of food for their family, and that was just the basics that they had to have. Which was flour sugar, salt, and lard etc. They all sat down to eat, and then they all bowed their heads and said grace. Everyone was hungry so Priscilla helped her younger siblings who sat beside her dish out their food on their plates. Her brother Joseph was the funny one that they always laughed at, at the table. He would always dive in to eat and right now his face was already smeared all over with pizza sauce. He did not really seem to care for the toss salad her mom had put in a little plate for him. He was more interested in the sauce on the pizza and the topping. Priscilla herself thought the pizza was really good tonight. The warmness of the heat that came from the wood stove that had been stoked to bake, and the warm tempature from outdoors made her drousy. The windows were open and there was a nice breeze floating in that felt really good and relaxing to her. She could see the pine trees surrounding the house waving their branches as the wind softly blew through them. Their house was simple but the warmness of their family bond made it seem luxurious. It did not take long until everyone seemed stuffed and full. Her dad got up and went over and sat in his chair and started reading the newspaper that he had got on his way home from work. Her mom continued to finish her sewing that she had to do by hand. Priscilla got up and cleared the table and put all the dishes in the sink. She got the bucket of water beside the sink on the floor and poured it in a basin. She figured it was ok to use cold water tonight to do the dishes because the dishes were not sitting there long. She put in some soap and started scrubbing. Before she knew it all the dishes were clean and she was almost done. She took her dish rag and wiped off the table and that was all she had left to do. She did not ask her sisters to wipe the dishes dry because she knew wiping dishes when they were washed with cold water was not easy. She just left them there to dry on the drainer rack and decided it was easier and that it did not hurt anything. She headed outside to see what her sisters were up to. As soon as they were done eating they had run out the door. She assumed they did not want to get asked to help with the dishes, and tonight they had got their wish. She found them crawling up their biggest pine tree that was in front of their house where their homemade swing was attached to. She told them to get down because it was quite high and a little dangerous. They complained and did not want to, but they did what she told them too. She knew they thought that she was bossy sometimes, but they also knew that she was older and usually if they did not listen,Priscilla would get her mom or dad and then they were really in trouble. Priscilla told them if they got on the swing they could take turns and then she would push them really high. Her sisters decided that sounded like fun so they both ran for the swing. Priscilla laughed because now she had created another problem. Her sisters Loretta and Emma were now arguing who could go first. She told them to hold out their hands and then she did the Tic Tac Toe game to see who's hand she counted last. It was Emma that she counted last, so Emma got to swing first. Priscilla pushed her higher and higher, and soon Emma was going really high, and laughing with delight. After about five minutes she stopped and gave Loretta a turn. Her brother came running out while Loretta was still swinging and wanted to swing too. He was too small to be on it alone so after Loretta was done, she sat on the swing and told him to come and then she sat him on her lap. She made them go by pushing with her feet. After about five pushes they were getting quite high and her brother was squealing and waving his hands. Priscilla laughed with him and held him tightly. After a couple minutes of swinging Priscilla decided she wanted to go inside and read her book she had been reading in the last few days. She gently put Joseph down on the ground and told her sisters to make sure he stayed with them if they wanted to stay outside and play. Loretta and Emma assured her they would. When she got in the house her dad was reading and her mom was doing some hand sewing near a kerosene lamp that her momwould light in the evening. She hurried over to the ladder and almost ran up it. She went to her room and flopped down on her bed with a happy sigh. She loved how the wind was blowing in her open window and her curtain was slightly fluttering. The wind smelled nice and fresh with it's summery breeze. Her book was still on her pillow where she had left it last. She grabbed the book and laid on her back and opened it to where her bookmarker was from where she had left off reading last. Her bed was soft and bouncy and felt good to her somewhat tired body. It did not take long until she was lost in her book. She was in a whole different world for about a hour when all of a sudden she heard her mom calling her to go bring her sisters and brother inside and ready for bed. She closed her book with a regretful sigh because she had just got to the most interesting part. Oh well she said to herself. She reminded herself that she had another day ahead of her tomorrow to read that part. She headed downstairs and climbed off of the ladder. When she got out the door she saw they were done playing in the sandbox and by now they had found some string and were pretending they were driving a horse. One of her sisters was in front being the horse, and the other was driving and telling her when to go and stop. Her brother was just running behind waving a stick he had found and saying "go horsey". She told them it was time for bed and to come inside. Her oldest sister Loretta said they would be right in, so Priscilla went inside and proceeded to fill a basin of water to wash their faces, hands and feet in before they crawled into bed. Her dad and mom were sitting on the couch talking about what happened today. Her dad told them to come over so they could all say a prayer before bed. After they had all washed up she helped her brother upstairs,and her sisters followed her. The curtains from her bedroom window were fluttering from the wind blowing through her open window. She took her brother over to her bed and sat him on it, and then told her sisters to gather around her bed if they wanted to hear a bedtime story. Her sisters always liked to hear a story especially at night when they had nothing better to do. Her sisters excitedly jumped on her bed and propped their head up with a hand on their chin. She began telling them of a young boy who always liked to do things his parents told him not too, and how one day he crawled out of his bedroom window and climbed down a tree to run over to his next door friends house. She told them this boy was five and his friend lived just down the road and by the time he was halfway there he met a big gray wolf who chased him all the way home and by the time he got back to his parents door the wolf had ahold of his pants and pulled them off so he had to walk in without his pants and explain to his parents what he did. She told them never to do something like that because their are wolves out there just ready to eat children when they are bad. Her sisters eyes got big and they said they don't want to get off her bed to go to their bed. Priscilla told them they were being silly because wolves don't live in peoples houses. Her sisters giggled and ran to their bed making sure their feet were off the floor as soon as possible. Her brother had fallen asleep mid story and was snoring with his head on her lap. She slowly got up and carried him over to his room and put him in his bed. She quietly tiptoed away making sure he was still sleeping and left the door to his room open. Seeing that he was still sound asleep she went to her room across the hall and crawled into her bed. It felt good to lay down in her soft bed and let all her muscles relax. It had been a eventful day. She was thinking things over that had happened that day and before she knew it she had drifted off to sleep. She awoke with the sun shining in through the cracks of her window. She was still slightly sleepy so she yawned and rolled over to catch a few more moments of relaxation. It did not last long before her mom was calling her name from downstairs. With a sigh of obedience she slowly got out of bed. Her sisters were still sound asleep. Sometimes she almost envied them because they were allowed to sleep in since they were younger than her and having that privilege. Oh well she reasoned to herself that at least she was older and could do more on her own. She guessed that every aspect of life had bad and good advantages to it. She looked in the mirror and when she saw her hair she laughed. She imangined right now she could pass for a animal in the jungle. Her hair was thick and tossing in her sleep at night would make it all bunch up high on the top of her head. Her window was still slightly cracked from last night so she could catch a cool breeze since at night it had been fairly warm. Her curtains were just moving from the wind every so slightly. The morning air smelled fresh and dewey. She picked up her comb and tried to work some order in her disarray of hair. After about 5 minutes she managed to comb her hair to the way she thought looked nice and neat. She took of her nightgown and found a clean dress in her closet. She quickly slipped it on and then went over to look out the window. The smell of the pines where really fragrant this morning. She loved how their branches were waving in the wind with the sun just starting to rise right above them. She knew that she had better get moving faster or her mom would call her a second time to make sure she was up. Sometimes she wished she could rise whenever she wanted too and do stuff at her own pace, but then she probably would be way behind and breakfast would probably be late she thought to herself. She went over and told her sisters that it was time to get up. It usually took them a while to get up anyway so she figured she might as well wake them now. She peeped in her brothers room. He was still sound asleep so she headed down the ladder that they called their stairs. Her mom as usual was already busily making hot cereal mush on the stove. Her mom handed her the egg container and told her to hurry and gather the eggs in the chicken house so they could have them for breakfast. They also gathered eggs at night but sometimes there were not enough eggs or they would use them to bake something so they would need more. A few of their hens had it in their head to hide a nest of eggs outside of the chicken house in the woods so they could try and hatch them. All the chickens knew though that if at night at dusk they did not roost in the chicken house sometimes a wild animal would sneak up. One evening when Priscilla had gone too late to close up the chicken house she had seen a racoon amidst the chicken house doing his best to grab one. But when he saw her he had relectulantly ran but not as fast as she wanted him too. All the raccoon had got that night was a few feathers but it had made Priscilla feel guilty and helped her to not forget her job of shutting the door as soon as the earliest sign of dusk was near. She liked the path out to the chicken house in the morning because she loved to hear the birds chirping beside her in the woods. The only thing she did not like and was always alert for was a snake. She entered the chicken house and searched the nests for eggs. She found about 8 eggs and put them in her basket. The chickens laid about a dozen a day and sometimes more, but since they had gathered them last night she only had eight this morning. She headed back to the house enjoying the view of the tall trees beside her path and the sun streaming through it. When she entered the house she saw her sisters were already up and even her little brother was already sitting in his high chair looking anxious to eat. The cornmeal mush her mom had made was on the table on a thick potholder and hot steam was seeping through the lid. Priscilla handed the eggs to her mom who already had the cast iron frying pan on the stove and hot and ready for the eggs. She grabbed the pail they used for fresh drinking water from the spring without being told and hurried up her usual morning path. The grass beside the trail was still wet with dew but the air was already getting warm as the sun was progressing further. She decided it took too long to just walk so she started skipping along the well worn path. The weeds and grass beside her were almost as tall as her, but the path was used so much there was like almost no grass on it at all. She wondered what today would bring. Her dad as usual would be going to work at the mine and her mom probably would be sewing for the people who brought her clothes to be mended from days before. She liked most of the people who brought clothes to be mended because they were friendly and sometimes would stay a little to talk and visit. Every once in awhile a old timer who looked worn out and grumpy would bring his tattered clothes to be mended. Her mom would try to carry on a happy conversation with the person, but usually would only get a few words in reply. She had reached her destination now so she quickly filled the bucket with fresh water bubbling from the spring. She shifted the bucket to her right arm and started on her way back. With the bucket heavy on her hand there was no skipping on the way back, but that did not defuse her happy thoughts and ideas for today. When she finally got back to the house her dad was washing up and all her siblings were already seated at the table except for Loretta who was putting the last pieces of silverware on the table. Loretta was beginning to get more helpful every day Priscilla had noticed. It sure helped her out when Loretta pitched in to help. Her mom put the fried eggs on the table along with a platter of fresh homemade bread and all was set. Her dad dried off from a hand towel and sat down at the table. Priscilla saw her mom had already strained the fresh warm milk her dad had brought in and put it in a pail of cold water to cool. Her dad told them to bow their heads and they said grace. Everyone seemed to be in a good mood today and hungry. Priscilla could not deny that she was hungry as her stomach was already growling from all the excerise she had,had this morning. The eggs were passed around and Priscilla loving homemade butter spread as much butter on her bread as she dared to before someone would tell her to be scarce with it. Butter was a chore to make sometimes and there never seemed to be to much of it. They would let a pail of milk sit for at least 15 minutes then they would scoop off the cream on the top and then put it in a jar with a lid put firmly on the top. They would then take turns shaking it in the jar until the cream would seperate and form into butter. They would save the buttermilk for baking. The buttermilk made really good pancakes. After the corn mush was passed around and everyone was full, her dad got up and told them all to be good children today for her mom and said good bye. Then he headed out the lane driving their rattly old car leaving a trail of dust following behind him. Priscilla could not help but wonder how it would be to work in a underground mine. She figured she probably would not really enjoy it but she still could not help wondering and imangining about how it would be. Her sisters were helping each other clear off the table as Priscilla was preparing the water in the sink to wash the dishes. Her mom went over to her big pile of sewing and sat down by her sewing machine. Soon her mother started pushing the treadle of the sewing machine with her feet to sew a long seam of clothing. Her brother was standing beside her mother fasinated by the whirring sound of the treadle and the sound of the needle going up and down. Priscilla put the big pile of dishes in her water to soak and meanwhile she was in deep thought looking out the window in front of her. She was thinking of something she could do today that would be a exciting new venture. She had already made a hammock, and a raft on 2 big barrells that supported her weight and she was still waiting on the herb guy to pick up her goldenseal that she had found in the woods and dried by herself. The herb guy came around just every so often. She started scrubbing the dishes vigoriously anxious to get them over and done with. Dishes in her household seemed like a never ending job. But they all loved to eat she thought to herself. Her sisters helped dry a stack of dishes and when they saw the rest would fit on the rack of the drainer to dry they ran outside to play. After Priscilla was done with the dishes she went outside to see what they were doing. Loretta was busy playing in the sandbox and Emma was swinging on the swing. Priscilla went over to show Loretta how to make a huge tall tower with sand. After Emma saw the tower beginning to get tall that Priscilla was making she came over and wanted to be part of it too. Soon it was all three of them competing with each other. Of course Priscilla being older seemed to be better at building a big sand tower. After Priscilla had made it as tall as she coulld without it crumbling down she laughed and told them it was theirs to play with now. Her sisters did not take long to argue who could have it and before she knew it in their arguement they accidentally knocked the whole thing down. Her sisters looked at it in dismay and then they started giggling. Priscilla decided to go for a walk. She went past the garden and saw it was getting a lot of weeds again but she did not feel like weeding it right now. She felt like building something. She went inside the barn and looked around at her dads scraps of odds n ends of lumber laying around. All of a sudden she had an idea. She always loved tree house and trees. She had an idea all formed in her mind. She felt the rush of excitement that she always felt when she thought she had just stumbled across a great idea! She saw a hammer hanging on the wall and after looking around for awhile she found some nails. She knew she had better not use her dads brand new nails so she looked around for some used ones. Sure enough over on a shelf were some old nails that were all rusty. Now all she needed was some short pieces of wood that she could nail against a tree to make steps for her to climb up a tree. She picked up a handful of one foot long small boards and her nails and went looking for the perfect tree. She knew she had better pick one out of of her parents sight because they might not approve of her building skills. She walked a couple steps and then she spotted a tall tree filled with branches and leaves around it. Yes she said to herself this is perfect! It was so lush with branches and leaves and also other trees surrounding it that it would be a great hiding place! She ran over and piled her stuff beside her tree then went back in the barn to get the hammer. Her parents were so busy that they would never even notice it unless they went for a nice walk. The woods around there house and beyond were so thick and wooded that it was easy to hide something like this. She found the hammer she was looking for and filled with excitement and a sudden new energy she hurried back to her spot. It did not take long until she was busy at work. After a half hour of work she already had 12 boards nailed for her steps on the tree and decided that should be high enough for her to start looking for bigger pieces of wood or boards to make her platform for her treehouse. She assumed it was about 12 feet high so that should do it. She went and walked around the barn and her dads storage shed looking for the right pieces. Her dad was always building something in his spare time so there were plenty of boards laying around but she just needed the right sizes. After searching for a bit she glimpsed a big square piece of a board about 3 feet wide and four feet long a couple feet from her.She ran and picked it up. She decided that was probably the best one yet so she picked it up and took it over to her tree house. It was about an hour now so she decided she had best go back and see what the others were doing before she finished her project. It was not good if she stayed away too long and her mom would have to come looking for her. She knew her mom would not be happy if she had to take off from her work to look for her and besides she was supposed to watch out for her younger siblings. She found her sisters playing with some twigs and making little pretend houses with them. Her brother was outside too and Loretta had been told to watch him by her mother she told Priscilla. Priscilla knew it would not be long until she would have to help her mom prepare lunch. She went inside to see what her mom was doing. Her mom was taking a break and reading a newspaper. Priscilla asked her mom what they would be having for lunch. Her mom told her to pick some tomatoes and lettuce and they would have that with some venison stew that they had canned last winter. Her dad was very good at hunting and had shot a deer last winter for their family. Priscilla knew she still had 2 hours until lunch so she went back outside and made sure her sisters and brother were busy playing and safe then she ran for her tree house she was making. She picked up the square board for her platform and stuck some nails in her dress pocket and balancing her board and hammer in one hand she used the other hand to climb. She was trying to be as careful as possible but it was hard. It went through her mind that maybe this is why she did not tell her mother, because her mother would worry. But she was a kid and she loved to do stuff like this. The fact that nobody knew she was doing it made it even more fun for her. After she reached the top slowly but surely she took the board and stacked it against the top step and the tree and with the hammer under her arm she pulled out a couple nails. Balancing everything up that high was not easy. She stopped a moment to think what would be the best way to do it. Having it all planned out she carefully put the board as tightly against the tree and the top step as she could and got the hammer and nails and nailed it on each side. It was not very stable but she knew what she had to do. She knew she needed 2 braces that were very sturdy and strong to hold each side up. After carefully climbing backwards down the tree on her steps that she had nailed against the tree she went to the barn where she remembered seeing a couple of 3 foot long boards. She got 2 of them and hurried back. Carefully balancing her boards and herself she climbed back up the tree.

It was almost painstakingly hard to climb and carry but she managed it. Now all she had to do was put the two braces on with one on each side. She put the first one on and made sure it was evenly against the tree and under the square platform then she pounded a couple nails in the tree and the platform. She did that to the other side too, then stood back a little to admire it. She took her hand and wiggled it and she was surprised what a difference those 2 boards for braces had made! She knew she had better head to the garden and pick the vegetables her mom told her to get before lunch. She felt proud of her accomplishment. The green leaves all around her up high looked absolutely beautiful and heavenly to her. It was a simple treestand but it worked for her for now. She assumed when she had more time sometime she could make some improvements to it. She climbed back down and looked at it one more time and she had the happy feeling that this was definately going to make her day! She grabbed the hammer and the rest of the nails and ran in the barn to put them exactly where they had been before. She knew her dad liked to have his tools right where he put them. Then she headed for the garden. When she reached the garden she found several really red and beautiful tomatoes. She always liked to pick the prettiest ones and marvel at their perfection. She grabbed a few handfuls of lettuce in one hand and with 3 tomatoes in the other she went in the house to help make lunch. Her mom had already sliced bread and also had stew heating on the stove. She knew she had to make another trip to the garden to get more lettuce. So she got a bowl from under the sink and a cutting knife and went back out to the garden. She held the lettuce at the very top and quickly cut beneath until her bowl was almost full. Then she found the row of onions and also radishes and added them to her bowl too. Heading back to the house she could hear her sisters laughing and yelling to each other in fun. She found them chasing each other around the house with her brother trying to keep up as fast as his little feet would go. She was glad they were having fun because it seemed to her that fifty percent of the time they were having a arguing contest about something. Laughing at their antics she went in the house. Her mom was looking out the doorway watching her sisters and brother as she came in the house. Her mom told her to wash the lettuce and other vegetables she had brought in and put them on the table. Priscilla did as she was told. The venison stew smelled good to her nose. Her mom was putting the stew on the table just as Priscila had finished up washing the vegetables and putting them on a big platter. Everything was ready and Priscilla was hungry so she went to the door and hollered at her sisters that it was time to eat now. Her sisters did not take long to come running. She went to help her brother out of the sandbox where he had just been playing. She brushed off his feet that were covered with sand and picked him up and carried him inside while balancing him on her hip. She put him on his highchair and latched his chair to his little tabletop. Her sisters were washing their hands and faces in a basin of water her mom had prepared for them. After they were all ready they sat down at the table and said grace. They all had a nice bowl of steaming hot stew from the pot that they passed around. Because it was so beautiful out her mom said they could fix their sandwiches and eat outside. Priscilla fixed her brother and herself a sandwich and then headed ouside with him holding her hand. Her sisters were still inside finishing fixing their sandwich so she sat her brother down with her on the picnic table where they would sit to eat most of the summer during the daytime when her pa was not home. She thought to herself how nice it was to eat outside with the smell of the pine trees and the soft breeze of the wind. Sometimes the house got to hot for comfort when they used it to cook and bake their food. She was busy thinking about her new treestand. It was nothing fancy but just the idea that she could climb up it and that she had done it all by herself was fasinating and fun for her. She wondered how long it would take for her sisters to notice it. She guessed they would probably never find it until maybe years later when they were older, because it was quite aways away from the house and kinda hidden with all the trees they had surrounding their property. It woud be a good peaceful spot for her to go and just relax at times she thought to herself. After her sisters came outside they sat down with her to eat their sandwich too. It did not take long for them to decide they want to go play with still half of their sandwich in their hand. Oh well they are just children Priscilla thought to herself. She figured it would not hurt anything to just let them have fun. Her stomach felt full now and she even felt a little drowsy. She felt like going to her room and relaxing and doing a little of reading in her book that she was interested in. She told her sisters to make sure to keep an eye on her brother and then she went inside. She piled all the dishes in the sink and soaked them in cold water so later they would not be so hard to wash.

Her mom had returned to her sewing but she told Priscilla she was going to take a nap in a few minutes. Priscilla assured her mom that she would do the dishes later and headed upstairs. When she reached her bed she flopped down. She really liked how her bed felt when she was tired or wanted to relax. Her bed was very soft and bouncy. After taking a few deep breaths and enjoying the breeze coming from her open window and looking at the ceiling while laying on her back she reached for her book. Soon she was lost in her book and almost forgot where she really was. After a little while her eyes started to get tired and before she knew it she fell asleep. She barely even knew she was sleeping when she awoke with a start. One of her sisters had come in her room and told her that her mom wanted her to go help with the dishes. Priscilla told her she would come down soon. With a sigh she slowly rolled got out of her bed. The sun was in it's afternoon rays she could tell just by looking out her window. A bird was noisily chirping outside her window like it was trying to tell her that she had missed out on something. Priscilla rubbed her eyes and then headed over to the stairs. She slowly climbed down and went over to where the dishes were still piled in the sink. Her mom was back at her sewing. Priscilla got hot water off the stove from a tea kettle and poured it in her bowl full of dishes and added some soap too. She started scrubbing them and swished them through the rinse water and put them on the drainer to dry. Her mom had told Loretta and Emma to wipe the dishes so they were already standing there towel in hand. It did not take Priscilla long to wash the dishes since she was pretty fast at it. After they were all done and put away she noticed the floor had to be swept. She headed to get the broom and dustpan and started sweeping. Sweeping was pretty easy for her and it was amazing to her what a difference it made to the house just by sweeping the floor. After everything looked nice and clean she asked her mom if she could go outside. Her mom told her she could but she would have to keep an eye on her younger siblings. Priscilla assured her that she would and told them to go outside with her. They all headed out with her and soon Priscilla had them playing a game of tag with each other. She waited until they were happily playing and then she sneaked out back behind the barn in the trees to look at her tree house again. It was still there of course, but she just wanted to try it out one more time. Quickly she climbed up the steps she had nailed to the tree. After she had climbed all the way to the top she carefully climbed on the platform. She could see pretty far from there. She noticed that she could actually see her brother and sisters playing from here but they could not see her because she was high up and surrounded by leaves. This was fun and exciting to her. It was like she had a secret all her own. After sitting there for about 10 minutes just enjoying the leaves and the view she knew she should go back and play with her younger siblings. Relectulantly she crawled back down. Her sisters had barely even noticed she had left because by now they were playing with sticks and playing house again. Loretta even had a makeshift broom made from a stick and she was sweeping her house she had marked off and pretending the dirt floor was a real house. Emma seeing her do that was trying to do the same. Her brother was just watching all of it while patiently sucking his thumb. Priscilla knew it was almost time for her dad to come home from work so she headed inside to see if her mom needed her for anything. Her mom was taking a break and sitting in the rocking chair writing a letter to one of her friends who lived far away. Priscilla was still to young to know how it would be to grow up and move far away and write letters but she assumed maybe someday that would happen. She asked her mom if she needed her and her mom told not yet but in about half an hour she wanted her to peel potatoes for supper. Priscilla got their big stainless steel bowl and went out to their underground cellar to get some potatoes. That is where they would keep their potatoes after they dug them up in the fall. It was amazing to Priscilla how long they would actually last after being put in the underground cellar. She hated going in it though because it was dark and had spiderwebs on the inside and smelled dark and scary to her. She slowly opened the door making sure their were no snakes around or in it. It was hard to tell though because she did not have a flashlight or light inside and with just the door open she could see the potatoes but not the ground around the edghes.It was shadowy. She took a deep breath stepped in and grabbed some potatoes. Making sure she had enough to fill her bowl as quick as she could she filled it, then she ran back outside the underground cellar and shut the door and breathed again. This was certainly not her favorite job but she knew she had to do it. Following the path back to the house she was thinking to herself that she was glad this was done! She went inside and poured water on the potatoes to make them easier to peel. Then she got out her paring knife and started her job of peeling them. She heard the rattle of her dads car come in the long driveway that came to their house. Her family was always glad to see her dad come home. Her dad always had some kind of new news to tell them about the new storys or gossip in town. She heard the car stop and looked out the window and saw him jump out and pick up one of her sisters and toss her in the air. She looked closer and saw it was Emma. Emma was laughing and giggling. The girls usually liked whe he did that. Of course her dad did not toss them very high, but just enough so they would laugh. Her dad picked up her little brother who could not wait to be held and came in to talk to mom. Priscilla hurried up and peeled the potatoes as fast as she could. Finally she was done. She cut them up in little pieces and put them in a big pot with water on the stove to start cooking, She checked the stove and saw it needed more wood so it would cook faster. She went outside and got more wood from the wood pile near the house and lifted the oven door and put it in. Some sparks flew out but that was it. Soon she heard the stove start up. She figured that was good now her potatoes would cook faster. Her mom and dad were talking about their days work. They were both sitting in their easy chair talking. Her mom was sewing something by hand on her rocker and her dad was sitting in his easy chair talking with her brother still on his lap. She heard her dad say that today the had got a lot of work done in the mines but that they had to be very careful because sometimes things could go wrong. Her mom of course like always was worried but told him she knew he would be careful. Her dad was saying his crop of corn back in the fields was doing very good this year and he had high hopes for it. He would usually take a week off in the fall to harvest all his crops and also a week in the spring to put everything in the ground. Priscilla loved to watch things grow so she would usually watch him harrow and plant crops with their big belgian horses that her dad had to help with the work in the fields. She liked to work in the garden too, but sometimes she got tired of hoeing and pulling weeds that seemed to come from nowhere and were never ending. Their corn in their garden was about ready to harvest too. It was so tall that sometimes her sisters would play hide and seekin it. Priscilla told her sisters to come inside and set the table to get it ready for supper. They came but not right away. They always argued who's turn it was to set the table and who did the most. Priscilla usually just laughed at them and told them they were being silly. The potatoes were cooking now so Priscilla got out a fork and stuck it in a potato to see if it was soft. It was almost soft enough but not quite. She waited a few more minutes and then got some heavy duty potholders and picked the pot up from the stove and carried it over to the sink. Cracking the lid very slightly she dumped out all the water and then got out the potato masher and started mashing them. The steam that had come from the pot was making her face break out in a sweat. Her mom came over and made the gravy on the stove which took just a few minutes. They were having mashed potatoes and gravy with some homemade stuffing and greenbeans from the garden that Loretta had picked earlier and brought in. After everything was ready and put on the table her dad put down the newspaper he had beed reading and came over and sat down at the table. Everyone was sitting there ready to eat by now. It seemed like they were always hungry as children so they never had a problem sitting down to eat. Her dad asked all of them how their day was and they all chorused that they had a great day and had fun. Priscilla could not help but think of the secret adventure she had, had today all by herself. The food was passed around and everyone dug in to eat. Priscilla was deep in thought and thinking of her own days events with all the chatter of her sisters and brother and her parents in the background of her mind. After everyone was done eating and putting their two cents in, her dad asked them if they were done and Priscilla looking around could see they all looked warm and stuffed. Her dad went outside to finish milking the cow and her mom went out to the garden. Priscilla asked her sisters to help her with the dishes and was trying to coax them and tell them it was not that hard. Her sisters did not like helping but knew they should. Priscilla helped them clear off the dishes on the table and then she got out the big basins they used in the sink to wash the dishes. With Priscilla vigorously scrubbing and swishing the dishes through the soapy water it did not take long to get it done. When the last dish was on the drainer she told her sisters they could go out and play. They ran outside happy to go with her brother following in tow. Priscilla hollered after them to make sure to watch out for him, and Loretta yelled back and promised she would. With a happy sigh she headed upstairs to relax in her room and read the interesting chapter of her book she was reading earlier today. Her window was open and the breeze coming through with the scent from the pines smelled so good and refreshing to her senses. Her curtain was fluttering ever so slightly from the wind. She sprawled on her bed and soon was lost in the exciting and alluring contents of her book. It did not seem like an hour until she looked at her clock in her room because she heard her mom calling her to go get her sisters and brother ready for bed. With a grunt she closed her book and rolled off the side of her bed. She climbed down the stairs and went outside only to find her sisters trying to chase the cow back in the pasture because she had gotten out. Her brother was right behind them waving his hands too. Priscilla helped them put her back in pasture and hooked the gate and then told them to come in the house with her. She helped them wash their faces hands and feet, and then her dad asked them all to come in the living room so they could say their prayers before bed. After the prayers were said they all raced each other to bed. Laying in bed that night Priscilla felt tired but happy at her accomplishment of the day. Her brother had decided to fall asleep next to her so she just let him be. As she drifted off to sleep she remembered thinking of what her next adventure would be.

The next she knew it was morning and she woke up to mom calling her name. She got up and grabbed her hair brush and brushed a few swipes through her hair and changed into a simple but pretty green dress. She looked out her window and saw the sun had already risen and was high up in the sky. The pine trees were standing there high and tall waving there branches in the wind like always. She peeked into her brothers room and saw he was awake so she went over and picked him up and carried him down the stairs. Her mom was cooking breakfast on the stove like usual. Priscilla put her brother down then she went over and picked up the pail to go get their daily drinking water from the spring. She walked outside and immediately noticed what a beautiful day it was. She trudged along the worn out trail on the grass from them getting their water every day. She heard the early birds already singing their songs from high up in the tree tops. She almost tripped over a killdeer bird trying to deter her from it's hidden nest. She laughed to herself thinking how furious and almost aggressive the killdeer was. It did not take her long to get to the spring. The water was gushing really vigoriously from underground this morning. She put her pail underneath the spout that they had put in to make the water pour out evenly and into a pail. It took only a few seconds for the pail to get full of water. She picked it up and started on her way back to the house. When her arm she carried the water with got tired she shifted it to the other hand. Her right arm could carry it a lot longer than her left hand she noticed. She could not help but wonder why. When she got to the house everyone was already washing up for breakfast. Everyone always washed in a basin in the sink because they only had a outdoors outhouse and no indoors bathroom. Their outhouse was outside and between that and their black kettle stood their outdoors tub where they bathed in. The outdoors bathtub was made as the same structure that their wringer washer building was. It had 4 posts and a tin roof on top and simple wood sides and the boards were nailed to each other along the sides. Usually if someone took a bath they would let each other know so they would not bother the one taking a bath. Priscilla quickly washed her face and hands and dried on a hand towel, then she sat down at the table where the rest of the family already were. Breakfast smelled great and Priscilla was hungry from the excerise she had just had. The corn meal cakes were passed around that her mom had fried. They put on brown sugar on them and added milk. She always liked hers soaked with milk so that it was very moist and soft. It had rained last night so the air coming through the windows was nice and fresh. After breakfast was over and the dishes were put away, she went outside to look what she could find to do to make her day fun. She always loved how some of her friends had a hammock, but her family would not buy one because that to them was a luxury. She had an idea how to make one of her own. She headed out to the barn where her dad had baler twine hanging around that was used once already. She found some hanging on a nail, and beside it was a whole roll of brand new ones all wound up. She got the the ones hanging on a nail and started unraveling them to straighten them out all in one single row. She took them with her and went back to the trees behind the house and sat down to concentrate on her idea. It took a while to line them all up and cut them with her jack knife to line up in a single row. Now she made them all the same length across of about 3 feet width until she assumed she had enough to make a hammock that would hold someone up to 6 foot tall. Next she cut the twine and tied them together into pieces of 6 foot length to tie them onto her other 3 foot length across. She just kept tying and tying until finally she could see that she was getting somewhere but not fast. She could see that her idea would probably work but she just had to patiently keep working at it. Her desire to have a hammock and the idea that she could actually make her own hammock kept her motivated to keep at it. After a half hour of work she heard her mom call her name so she hung up her work on a nearby tree and ran to see what her mom wanted. Her mom wanted her to watch little Joseph because he wanted to go out and play. She got Joseph and headed to the sandbox with him. Her sisters were in the house coloring pictures that they had drawn themselves off of scraps of paper. The only thing that made the sun seem less intense was the breeze coming through the pine trees. She showed her brother how to pile sand and make little squares and make houses so everyone can have there own house and a field to have cattle in. She broke twigs off of a nearby tree and stuck them in the sand to be the cattle. Her brother thought that was the fun part and he seemed quite entertained. Meanwhile Priscilla wanted to get her hammock finished so when she saw her brother was busy she ran and got her half finished work and brought it to the sandbox. She sat on the grass beside it and busily started weaving. It did not seem to take her too long before she looked at it and figured it was good enough to use. She stood up and excited to go try it out she asked her brother if he wanted to come watch her put it between two trees. Her brother babbled something and came running after her. She found two nicely shaded pine trees and proceeded to tie one end to the first tree. When she had that end securely tied she picked up the other end and finished wrapping the ends of the twine around the second tree. It was hard to keep her brother off it until she was done. She had added extra length to the ends on each side so she had enough to go around each tree. Now she was done and wanted to see if it held her weight and her brothers. She carefully climbed on it and even though it was a little flimsy and she swung to and fro for a little bit, it soon stopped and she told her brother to come and join her. She picked him up and put him on top of her, because their was no room beside her as the hammock had doubled up. . The homemade hammock swung back and forth with the added weight, and her brother thought that was fun. He was laughing and saying words about swinging. After about five minutes of being in the hammock her brother got restless and tried to get off. When he tried to get off of one side Priscilla was trying to help him, and in one split second they both where on the ground. It happened so fast she almost did not even know it happened. They both got up from the ground looking a little dizzy. What had happened she saw after examining the hammock was, that if you were on it you should not try to turn to just one side because it would just dump you right out. Her brother was not hurt just surprised and it did not take long for him to recover. Her brother started running to the house so she ran in tow. He went inside the house and in his own words was trying to tell her sisterswhat had happened. Priscilla did not really want her sisters trying out the hammock just yet so she acted as if she did not know what he was saying. She knew her sisters and with all the work she had put in it she figured they would see it and try it out soon enough. Her mom told her to take a knife and bowl out to the garden and cut the lettuce for lunch and also bring in some radishes carrots and onions. She found a sharp knife in the silverware drawer and got a big bowl and headed out. There was always plenty of lettuce in the garden. Her mom always pushed healthy foods on her children to eat. Sometimes Priscilla and her siblings would rather skimp on the vegetables and endulge in the fresh apple or cherry pie her mom had baked. They did have a cherry tree out back in their field, and they would take a ladder to put against the tree to pick them. They canned them for pie in the winter so they could not eat as many fresh as they wanted too.

She hurried and cut the lettuce and pulled out some radishes and carrots and one onion, and headed inside to wash everything for lunch. Her sisters were chasing each other around the table and her brother was watching her mom at the sewing machine. It was a somewhat quiet day especially with her father at the mine working. She thought maybe later today she would go for a ride in her raft on the river, or just simply read a book resting in her newly made hammock. She could smell homemade bread coming from the oven that her mom had put in the oven earlier. It smelled good and made her hungry. Bread was a big item in their house because it was easy to make and it seemed to fill their growing tummies quickly. They always loved to put butter or honey on some warm fresh bread. She washed up the lettuce and vegetables and put everything on the table. She checked the bread and sure enough it was read. She got some pot holders and got the 3 loafs one by one and dumped the loaves out on the counter to cool off. After letting them cool off for 10 minutes she sliced one loaf and put it on the table on a plate and put a jar of mayonaise and butter on the table and everything was set to eat. She told her sisters to grab a plate on the counter and help themselves, and then she set out to fix her brothers plate. Her brother was not a big lettuce eater so she just fixed him a sandwich with butter and honey on it and put some lettuce and tomato on the side. After they all had a plate fixed they went outside to eat. Her mom was still sewing but said she will eat soon. They sat outside at their picnic table on the lawn and started eating. Her sisters were being goofy and imanging they were rabbits chewing at their lettuce. They loved the tomatoe on their sandwich more than their lettuce. Her brothers hands and face were sticky from the honey but he did not seem to mind. All of a sudden Loretta noticed the hammock in the trees. Loretta said hey Emma look what is that? By then both of her sisters had took off racing to see who could get their first. Of course since Loretta was bigger and older she got their first. Loretta said, hey Emma sit in it and then she helped Emma get into it. Priscilla was just calmly eating her sandwich and garden salad and watching them. She had known that they would find it soon enough without telling them. She starting laughing when she saw Emma trying to get out and the hammock flopped upside down and she fell right out. She guessed the hammock was okay for laying in it but not for playing because it was just too flimsy. She started gathering up all their plates and took them inside. Her mom was taking a short nap so she just stacked the dishes in the sink and poured water over them so they would soak and be easier to wash later. She looked out the door and saw her sisters and brother were now playing in the sandbox so she decided to go upstairs to her room to read. She went up the ladder and saw how her curtain from her window was flopping in the breeze. She hoped that did not mean that it would rain until at least tonight. They all liked sunny days so thay could play outside. She threw herself on her bed and bounced back up. She looked out the window and noticed a airplane flying high up in the sky. She often wondered how it would be like to fly in one. Sometimes she just liked laying on her bed and looking at the ceiling and out her window dreaming of all the things she wanted to do some day when she grew up. Life seemed so full of things for her to still explore. She grabbed her book and began to read. She could feel the breeze coming from outside, and the pine trees sounded like they were whispering to each other. It did not take long until she forgot who she was, and she was busy being a detective in her book.

She was brought back to her own life shortly though by her mom calling her name to make some bread dough. She reluctantly closed her book and headed downstairs. She heated up some water on the stove and put one quart of luke warm water in their big stainless steel mixing bowl and soon she had it all mixed together and ready to set aside and rise. She covered it with a thin dish towel so no stray flies would land on it. She grabbed a bowl and garden cutting knife and went out to look at the garden. She loved how the garden looked this time of the year with everything looking so lush and green and at it's prime. The only thing that was not so alluring to her about having a big garden was when her mom would tell them to hoe the weeds. The sun in a south Carolina summer could be very warm sometimes. The lettuce was plentiful she noticed as she quickly cut off enough to half fill her bowl. She found the row of onions and proceeded to find the biggest one to take back inside for her mother. She found a huge one in the middle of the row. She pulled out a couple of radishes, and carrots, and headed back to the house with her bowl full of fresh garden vegetables. When she got back inside the house she saw the bread had risen now so she prepared and greased 5 pans. Next she greased her hands and got out enough dough to make one loaf. By greasing her hands it made that the sticky dough would not stick to her hands and it was easier for her to form a loaf and make it look nice and smooth. One by one she pounded the air out of a loaf and formed them then set them in a pan to rise once again before she would put them in the oven to bake. She went outside and found some twigs laying around and picked them up and took them inside and threw them in the stove to prepare it to get hot enough to bake the bread. Her dad would soon be coming home from work. It was a hot and humid day and she imangined her dad would be sweaty sticky and tired. Her mom had took a break from sewing and was reading the newspaper and sitting on the rocking chair rocking her little brother who was more concerned in trying to crumple his mothers paper. Priscilla got the 5 loaves of bread which by now were twice the size that they had been 10 minutes ago, and put them in the oven to bake. Perspiration was forming on her brow from the hot stove. The aroma of fresh bread was coming from the oven and as she went outside to see what her sisters where doing she noticed she could smell the bread from 20 feet away coming from one of the open windows. The pine trees had their own special scent that made the air outside smell so nice and fresh. She found her sisters outdoors arguing about how to play fair in their game of stacking up sticks that they had made of pine needles. Her sisters were telling each other that whoever got a pine needle without making the other pine needles fall could keep it until the one they got made the others fall, and whoever had the most when the game was over would win. It was quite funny to Priscilla to watch them because each was trying to win and when one did not win for awhile they got kind of huffy and it caused a debate. She saw her dad coming in the driveway so she ran inside. By then she saw the bread was brown and done, so she got a pair of pot holders and got them out. She washed and put the fresh lettuce in a bowl and put it on the table. Her mom had oyster soup on the stove that was hot by now so she picked that up and put it on a potholder on the table too. The oysters came from a can from the store and then the milk they got from their cow was added to make it oyster soup. Her dad came in and whistled and threw his hat on the rack beside the door and told them supper smelled really good! He washed his face and hands in a basin of water by the sink and then went over and teasingly lifted her mom in the air and put her back down so she could finish what she was doing. Her mom laughed and said she was glad he was in such a great mood. Then he went and sat down in his lazy chair to read the daily newspaper. Her brother was playing with a big cardboard box and crawling in it and acting like he had a little house of his own. Priscilla sliced the still warm bread and added it to the food on the table. Her mother said supper was ready so Priscilla ran out to tell her sisters to come inside. To her dismay she found her sister Loretta chasing Emma with a big squishy red tomato and it looked like Emma had already been plastered with tomatoes and even Loretta had some in her hair. Her sisters were both laughing. Priscilla told them to stop wasting tomatoes and to come inside to wash up for supper. They obeyed and raced each other inside. Her mom asked them what they had been doing, and her sisters said they were trying to see if they could hit each other with a tomato. Her mom laughed, but said that they needed the good tomatoes, and told them the next time they decided to do that to make sure it was only the rotten tomatoes that they had fun with throwing around and having a tomato fight. Priscilla helped her sisters wash off the tomato juice on their face and hands the best she could and then they sat down at the table. She pushed her brothers highchair over and then went and picked him up and sat him in it. Her mom told her dad to sit at the table because supper was ready, so he put his newspaper down that he was reading and came over to the table. Her mom sat down too and then they all bowed their heads and her dad said grace and thanked God for their nice little family. The oyster soup smelled good to their hungry tummies. When it was Priscilla's turn to dish out her soup she looked at the oysters and wondered why they smelled so good because she thought they looked really odd shaped and almost gross. But she was hungry so she decided to set those thoughts aside and eat. She reached for a piece of bread and put on some homemade butter and honey. That sure tasted and looked good to her. They had their own bee hive behind the barn so they would collect their own honey. When it was time to gather the honey her dad would put on a mask made of netting and make some smoke around the hive so the bees would stay away until he was done. She loved watching her dad gather the honey from the bee hive, but she was a little scared of getting stung so she usually kept her distance. Her dad was telling her mom what had happened that day, and then he said to her that tomorrow he had a day off from work and he had a little surprise for his family. Priscilla and her sisters ears perked right up. Her brother was too young to understand what was being said, so he just kept busily stuffing his face with the sllice of bread her mom had given him with his bowl of soup. Her dad started telling how he was going to give them all a little bit of money and see how wisely they would spend it tomorrow when he would take them to town. He said their first stop would be the new store that the new people in town had just opened up with all the furs and material to make clothes and some othe knick knacks. Priscilla was so excited after hearing that that she almost could not wait until tomorrow came. Her sisters eyes got big and they started telling their dad how happy they were, and assured him they would spend their money wisely. With her sisters talking with excitement her little brother seemed to catch on that something fun was in the air so he chimed in waving his hands and raising his voice in his own 2 year old babble to let everyone know he was in on whatever they were doing too. Her dad said if they were all good children they would all have a great time going for a nice ride to town tomorrow. Her mom seemed happy about it too and was smiling. When everyone was done eating, Priscilla got up with a smile on her face and since she was happy, doing the dishes did not seem like a chore to her at all. She quickly piled all the plates on top of each other and put them on the counter and got the basins full of water to wash them. She swished them vigorously tonight with energy that she did not know she had meanwhile singing a tune to herself. Her sisters helped her by wiping the dishes and even they seemed to get their work done tonight without a thought of who was wiping more dishes than the other. Soon all was done and the house was nice and clean. Her sisters went outside to play before dark and and their bedtime. They all liked to be outdoors or beside an open window when the sun started going down at night because in South Carolina the evenings were beautiful and the sunsets were colorful and pretty. Her brother seeing her sisters run out the door started following them as fast as his little feet would go. Priscilla went out with them, and told them she would push them on the swing. But she told them they had to take turns being pushed on their swing they had tied to a tree. It was tied to a huge tree and if she pushed hard it would go really high which her sisters loved. Her brother was young so one of them would hold him on the swing when it was his turn. The sun was starting to set and she saw it was almost time to get ready for bed. Her mom had told her to make sure the fire under the kettle was going and the water was hot before they washed up for bed, so that they could all be nice and clean for the next day. She told her sisters to keep pushing each other on the swing and see how good they were at it, then she headed out back to start the fire. She went in the house and grabbed some newspapers and some matches and went outside and put the newspaper under the kettle. Next she went to the nearby trees around their house and gathered some dry twigs that had fallen from the branches. She assumed these dry twigs would fire right up after she put them on top of the newspaper and lit them up. It just took a couple minutesand the fire was smoking and crackling. She stood back and looked at the fire with a sense of pride. She liked to think that she could start a fire under any circumstances. She was the oldest so she was responsible for a lot. Her dad had already filled the kettle with water yesterday when he had gone to the river nearby to get water for her mom to wash their clothes. She went and made sure the tub was ready and clean inside their simple bath area made of a tin roof and slabs of wood. The tub was not fastened to anything and everytime they changed the water they would stand it on one end and dump the water. The tub was still full of water from the last person who had took a bath so she used all of her strength and pushed the tub to the door and then stood it up on one end and dumped it out the door on the ground. Her mom often told her not to carry to heavy stuff and to dip out the water rather than dump it, but Priscilla always felt like it was much quicker and easier doing it this way. Plus she reasoned to herself she was saving time too doing it this way. She made sure their was soap on the stand beside the tub and a stack of wash cloths and towels. When she saw everything was ready and in place she headed out to see if the water was hot. She quickly stuck her finger in the top of the water of the kettle and withdrew it quickly. The water was lukewarm but she reasoned by the time she got her sisters and brother ready it would be hot. She headed to the front yard to find them and after searching she found them now the in the sandbox. Her sister Emma was complaining because her brother Joseph had just trampled her sand house by accident. Priscilla consoled her sister and told her it was ok and it was time to go take a bath anyway. She told her sister Loretta and Emma to hurry up and go to their bath house and to get their clean night clothes first. Her sisters did as they were told and ran to see who got ready first. Priscilla hoisted her brother Joseph up on her hip and headed outback to get the bathtub full of water. She put her brother down on a tree stump and told him to stay there while she went to get their 5 gallon bucket that they used to transport water from the kettle to their bath tub. She found it leaning against the building. She quickly dipped the steaming water out of the kettle without getting to near to the fire and poured it in the bathtub. She told her brother to follow her and headed towards the river to get cold water. Her brother glad he could get up, got off the stump and ran after her. The river was rushing wild today so she just stood at the very edge and dipped her pail in. She pulled the pail back out then took her brothers hand and headed back. She was beginning to feel tired from all the walking, lifting and carrying she had done in the past hour. When she got back she wearily poured the cold water in the tub to make it lukewarm and told her sisters they could jump in. Her sisters usually bathed together and then dump it. Then she would procede to fix her own clean bath water. They usually bathed twice a week since it was so much work to carry all their water and to always heat up their kettle water. But they would always wash their hands face legs and feet before they went to bed with just cold water. After all of them were clean and bathed they all got ready to go upstairs to bed. Her mom was done sewing for the night and her dad just came in the house with a pail of milk from their cow. Her dad washed up and came in the living room so they could all say their prayers before bed. After Priscilla crawled into bed that night she felt like her tired body sunk right down in the middle of her soft mattress. She could feel her muscles were sore and she remembered thinking what a job it was for all of them to just simply take a bath, before she drifted off to sleep. It was a great start to a new day and the sun was shining through the trees. She jumped out of bed happy for something new to happen today. Her dad had the day off from work and he had promised to take the family to the new store today. Going to town and being given money to buy something was something the whole family would talk for days about. Even though they had what they needed to get by and a home to live in money to them was scarce. They almost never had candy and the thought of picking out their favorite candy was thrilling to Priscilla and her sisters and brother. Priscilla was hoping she would have enough money left over for candy but what she wanted first and foremost was material to make a new dress. She had never sewed before, but her mom had promised her that when she was ready and old enough she could try the sewing machine. Watching her mom use the sewing machine looked like fun to her and just watching the needle go up and down really fast in a straight line intrigued her. When her mom sewed patches or clothes with a needle and thread it did not look quite as fun to her, but the sewing machine was a different story. She looked in the mirror and combed her hair nicely. Her hair was extra fluffy from the shampoo she had used the night before, so it was all puffed up from sleeping. She finished combing her hair, then she got one of her pretty hair ties and tied her hair in a neat pony tail. She found her prettiest simple dress and slipped it on. Now it was time to wake her sisters and help them get ready. She saw her sisters were still sound asleep, but because today was a special day she wanted to wake them up and get them ready for this special even. She nudged her sister Loretta and told her to wake up Emma too and then she went to her brothers room to get him dressed. Her brother was already awake and rubbing his eyes so she went in his dresser and got out his clothes. Her brother Joseph jumped out of bed ready to start the day. She gave him his pants and he started putting his legs in it but she had to help him pull them up. Next she put his shirt on and smoothed his hair and he was all set for the day. She went over and made sure her sisters were up and dressed and to her amazement they were nowhere in sight. She hoisted Joseph on her hip and headed downstairs. Her sisters obviously excited about today already had their favorite dresses on and even had combed their hair for once. Priscilla started setting the table and after she had that done she grabbed the pail to go get water from their spring. Her mom asked her sister Loretta to go gather the eggs out in the chicken house. On her way down the path Priscilla noticed how green the grass was and the dew on it made the grass wet. The birds were singing up in the trees and the same killdeer chased her that had set a nest near the path recently. It caught her by surprise and she jumped, but then she saw what it was and laughed at herself. She always forgot about it when she was lost in thought and then all of a sudden the killdeer would be right in front of her screeching at her in protest of her taking that path. She started skipping merrily down the worn path thinking of what a great day this would be. She saw the spring was just up ahead so she hurried up to it and her pail was fullbefore she knew it. She headed back to the house carrying the pail mostly in her right hand and switching it to her left when her right hand got tired. Halfway back lost in thought she almost dumped her pail as the same killdeer jumped out at her again. She was thankful she was in such a good mood because otherwise she would have been really irritated. When she got back to the house her dad was already done doing his chores and had his pail of milk on the counter beside the sink. Her mom had just set the corn meal mush on the table along with homemade maple syrup and brown sugar and milk from last nights milking that had been put in a pail of water to keep it cool. Priscilla got the cloth to strain the milk and then put a jug underneath and picked up the fresh pail of milk and slowly poured it in the jug. She could not pour it in too fast or it would overflow before it had a chance to go through the strainer. After the jug was full she set it aside and put on the lid and put it in a cold pail of water where it would be until someone had time to take it to the spring later. Her dad had already sat at the table, and told her other siblings to sit down too. Priscilla hurried and washed her face and hands and sat down at the table too. Her dad was telling the children that right after they all ate and did their morning chores, they would be leaving for town in their old town car. He said he was giving all of them two dollars and then he was going to be checking out their spending habits today. He also told them he would be disappointed if they spent all their money on candy. Her sisters eyes were glowing with excitement and everyone was happily digging in and eating their eggs. Their was corn meal mush on the table too, but this morning everyone seemed to excited to eat much. It did not take long for everyone to be done eating and with them being excited it seemed their tummies got full much quicker. Priscilla got up as soon as they were done and got the water ready to was the dishes. Her sisters for once were clearing the table without even being told. She scrubbed and swished the dishes in the soapy water and then rinsed them and put them on the drainer to dry. Her mom said it was ok to leave the dishes on the drainer to dry and they could put them away later, so Priscilla and her sisters went upstairs to touch up their hair one more time. When her sisters were satisfied with brushing their hair and how smooth their hair was they ran to see who got downstairs first. Priscilla told them to be careful because if they fell it would not be pretty. When she got downstairs her dad was handing her sisters their money. They took the two dollars and stared at it as if to make sure it was real, then put it in their pockets. Her dad handed her two dollars too and she looked at it and since it was the first time she had ever held a dollar she examined it closely. She put the money in her pocket feeling very grown up. She liked this feeling of power. She was allowed to spend her money on whatever she wanted too for once and that she thought was the best feeling ever. Her mom had brushed her hair and put it in a smooth and elegant looking bun at the back of her head with just wisps of hair dangling around her ears. Priscilla had never noticed how pretty her mother really was before, especially seeing her in a bright green dress that matched her eyes. Her dad had on a nice crisp blue shirt, and looked very dressed up compared to his usually dusty clothes he had grown used to working in a underground mine. She noticed how fluffy and clean his hair was, and that it was slicked back and nicely combed. He worked almost every day of his life and today was indeed a very special day for their family. Her sisters had tied a pretty bow in their hair that matched their pretty but simple dresses. Her brother had on his nicest shirt that was light brown and complimented his dark brown hair. She looked out the window and noticed how brigh and high up in the sky the sun was. The pine trees outside surrounding their house were waving in the breeze like they were happy too. With their windows open like always on a warm summer day like this she could smell the scent of the pines. She felt really happy because to her there was nothing better than her whole family being together and going to town to enjoy the sights of the town together. She liked the feeling of them all participating in an event together and right now she felt like she had the very best family in town. Her dad went out to start the car and the rest of them made sure they had everything they needed before their ride to town. Her mom had a jug full of lemonade and cups so no one would go thirsty and a loaf of bread and tomatoes and a jar of mayonaise. Priscilla helped carry the stuff out at the same time leading her little brother by the hand. Her brother not sure what was going on was doing his best at keeping up on his end. Her mom and dad sat in the front and she and her brother and sisters sat in the seat behind them, with her brother in the middle. After they were all seated her dad put the car in gear, and out the lane they went. The drive to town was about 40 miles so they had plenty of time to enjoy the scenery along the way. Priscilla loved to look at the trees as they went by, and she could not help but marvel at the beauty of nature and summer. The dirt road made a trail of dust that followed after them. They even saw a few deer grazing in the fields along the way. The sun was beating down so it did not take long until her mom had to get out the lemonade and cups. Of course everyone seemed to be thirsty at the same time so they had to patiently wait until their turn. The youngest ones got their drink of lemonade first and the rest waited for last. Her dad was whistling and striking up quite a conversation with all of them about what they were going to see and do when they got to town. Of course that only made them all the more excited. Priscilla thought the drive to town with all of them together as a family was so interesting and fun that she really was not in a hurry to have this day over at all. She told herself she was going to enjoy every minute of this day because this certainly did not happen all the time. A couple birds along the way fluttered as fast as they could to get out of their way, meanwhile the rest of the birds were chirping in the trees all around them. Her brother Joseph was squirming all over her and her sisters laps trying to get up higher so he could see better. Her sisters were having a conversation and trying to decide what was most important for them to spend their money on. Loretta and Emma both said they had to have at least a little of their favorite candy that they always wanted. Joseph heard the word candy and got all excited trying to repeat them. After what seemed like hours they finally got to the edge of town. Their where a lot of little shops and small houses along the road and also people selling fresh produce on the side of the road with cute little vegetable stands. Her dad had told them they were going to the new shop in town where they sold furs and clothing material and a lot of other stuff too. There was never a shop or store that they had been into that did not at least have a container of candy on the counter where they paid them for the stuff they got and they never forgot that. Usually the candy was five cents a piece and sometimes the owner of a store would give them a piece of candy for free and tell them that was just for being good little children. After about half a mile into town they spotted the new shop just up ahead. It looked very pretty from the outside and they could not help but wonder what was all inside. Her dad stopped the car beside the sidewalk and asked them if they were ready. Priscilla and her sisters and brother all chorused yes. Her dad said they all have to be good and can't take anything off the shelf without asking. Her mother and father went in first with her mom holding her brothers hand. Priscilla followed with her sisters in tow, and her youngest sister Emma holding her hand. It smelled like freshly cut trees inside, and she could see that the structure of the building by the look of the boards were still new. Their was a big rack of furs on one side of the store with all different kinds of fur that she had never seen before. There were fur hats, mittens, and coats and the rest she did not recognize. She saw all kinds of items like sparkling colorful little dishes and big rolls of material to make clothes and other stuff out of. Since she wanted a new dress she went over and started eyeing the material stacked against the wall wrapped around what looked like a strong piece of cardboard three feet long. There were so many pretty colors she almost could not decide what color was the prettiest. She could not take her eyes off of the light but bright green material though because it was such a fresh nice color. She went and touched the material and after feeling how soft it was she knew that was the one she wanted. She knew she only had two dollars so she began looking for the price of the material. She found the price on the corner of the cardboard and it read fifty cents a yard. She knew she needed about two and a half yards so she was delighted she had enough and even fifty cents left over. Her dad was talking to the store owner and her mom and sisters and brothers were looking at the furs. Her mom saw Priscilla looking at the material and came over to her side. Her mom asked her if she found what she was looking for and she happily said yes and showed her the price. Her mom helped her take the material over to the counter so the store owner could cut it. The sore owner asked her if that was what she wanted and she shyly said yes. She was not used to being around new people she had never met before so she was shy about meeting them. The store owner cut the material the length Priscilla told him to and after she handed her money to him he handed her the material and said good luck. Her sisters came over to the counter and were looking at the big jars of candy on the shelf with anticipation in their eyes. Her sister Loretta was holding her brother Joseph up so he could look at the candy too. Her brother of course got all excited and wanted to get closer but her sister knew better and put him back down on his feet. The jars of candy were all different and all of them were five cents a piece. Her mom asked her sisters if they needed help with what they were going to buy and they said yes. Loretta said she wanted the cute little china set with red roses on it to play with her dolls with, and Emma decided on a cute little sparkling blue dish to put on her nightstand and maybe even put her candy in she said. Her brother was too young yet to make his mind up on his own so her mother was carrying him around and showing him things. Her brothers eyes caught on a carved horse made out of wood, and he yelled "horsey" so her mom got it off the shelf for him and he held onto it tightly with his eyes shining with happiness. Her dad in the meantime had picked up a fur hat and her mom decided on some fur mittens. Priscilla and her sisters and brother ended up spending the rest of their money on the candy that they just could not resist going home without. Priscilla had got the some pink gumballs and a nice big red and white sugar cane. Her sisters had picked out some maple candy and gum and her brother had already put his candy cane in his mouth and his hands were already sticky. Her dad visited with the store keeper and they were talking about furs and what they really were worth in the trapping business. She was happy her dad had a day off and it seemed so unusual to see him all dressed up and just being able to spend time with their family on a beautiful day like today and doing something as special as this. Her mom was in a good mood and seemed to be glowing with happiness too. This was exactly like she liked it, with her family together and everyone enjoying each others company. Her dad thanked the owner of the store and they all headed back out to their car with their newly bought treasures in hand. They all sat down in their seats with Priscilla holding onto her brothers hand to help him get up on the seat. Her dad started up the engine and they were on their way to stop at some roadside markets just up the road. The first market they came too had big boxes of beautiful shiny apples and grapes. Priscilla and her sisters and brother loved grapes so her mom bought a pound of them. They were all getting hungry so her dad said they would find a nice shady tree near the river that flowed beside the road just a half mile from where they were. The sun was warm and they were thirsty and the grapes her mom had bought looked really good. It took them only a few minutes to get there and right there was the tree her dad had been talking about. It was a nice huge oak, and the river's water was rushing right beside it. It was a very pretty spot to eat the lunch her mom had packed Her dad stopped the car on the side of the road and Priscilla and her sisters excited to eat and not wanting to wait any longer than they had too jumped off to help her mom set up their picnic lunch. Her mom laid down the blanket she had brought for them to sit on and laid it on the grass underneath the tree. Her two sisters and brother had already found their seat on the exact spot they wanted on the blanket and were trying to patiently wait for their food. Her mom was fixing the sandwiches and Priscilla got the already sliced tomatoes ready to put on them. The lemonade was poured out in a cup for each of them. Her dad was looking at the scenery and the river, but after he saw they had all their sandwiches he came over and took his. Priscilla really loved the sound of the river and watching it while she ate was even better. The water was so crystal clear rushing over the rocks that if the sun shone in one exact spot it looked like the water had a little rainbow in it. Her parent's were busy talking so after she was full she went over to the river and stuck her feet in it. The water was cold compared to the warm summer day. Her brother seeing her do that came running after her wanting to play with water too. She let him wade in it but held his hand so he would not slip. Her sisters were still arguing over who gets the last sandwich so her mom cut it in half so they could each have one. Her sisters happy they each got half grabbed their sandwich, and spying Priscilla and her brother splashing in the river they ran over too. Priscilla told them to be careful because the rocks were slippery and if they went out to far they might get carried into the rivers current.

Her parent's where sitting back under the shade tree watching them and talking. After seeing Priscilla was watching her younger siblings her dad laid on his back with his hat flopped over his face to take a short nap. Her mom was putting the stuff they had left in containers and putting it back in their car. After everything was all nice and tidied up, her mom joined her dad on the picnic blanket, and after telling her kids to be careful, she decided to relax under the shade tree too. After about 15 minutes of her parent's napping under the shade tree her dad hollered over that it was time to go. They still had a long drive home and Priscilla knew it was getting later in the afternoon by now. After they were all in their seats off they started. Priscilla looked at the beautiful spot they had just been at until it got smaller and smaller and she could no longer see it. She was feeling a wee bit tired too now, but it was a happy relaxed feeling because today she had one of the best days that she could ever remember of. She wanted to stay awake on their ride home to see the beautiful scenery. The smell of summer and trees and the green grass was almost intoxicating to her. Her sisters had struck up a funny conversation of how they were going to use their items they had bought at the store and who they thought got the best gift. Of course her sisters both argued that their choice was the best. Loretta was telling her sister Emma, that her candy would last way longer than hers, and even though Emma had eaten more of her candy already she said that was not going to be true. Priscilla laughed at their competition, meanwhile she was thinking to herself how happy she was for her brand new material she had bought to make a dress. She just could not wait to try out the sewing machine her mother had for the first time. She reasoned in her mind that after they saw her with her pretty new dress they might think her choice was the best. She knew though that with the china set and the pretty blue dish that her sisters had picked out that they would have so much fun using when playing with their dolls. Soon she noticed the big maple tree that her dad had told them was the halfway mark on their trip to town. She could not help but notice how wide and tall the tree was. She looked up at the tree as high as she could and marveled at the thousands of leaves it had on it. The purring of the car and hearing her parents talking almost put her to sleep. Her brother was sound asleep by now and leaning against her. Her sisters on the other hand were still busy talking to each other. Priscilla was lost in thought and was just watching the beautiful scenery fly by. She saw a pond with ducks swimming in it, and not far down the road was a beautiful farm house with a big pasture that was fenced in with 2 beautiful brown horses who were taking a stroll in it. She really loved South Carolina and the beautiful summers there, but most importantly she had grown up there and loved where they lived. She was thinking about the raft she had made that she sometimes would take to the river to ride on the water, and how she could not wait for her mom to show her how to use her sewing machine to make her new dress. She had so much to think about that she did not realise they were almost home and before she knew it her dad had drove in their driveway. They were home so everyone jumped out of the car as soon as they could could carrying their prized possessions. Priscilla helped her brother off the seat and gave him his horse and then got her material. Her brother had woke up when her sisters had jostled him by jumping off their seat. She took her material up to her room so she would know where it was when she was ready to make her dress. Loretta came up the ladder behind her, carrying her china set, and Emma was right after her carefully balancing her blue dish made out of sparkling glass. They all wanted to make sure they took care of their stuff because they did not get this chance to get what they wanted very often. Joseph was too young to really understand, so he was downstairs gleefully playing with his new horsey. When Priscilla got back downstairs her mom was quickly trying to get supper ready as it was later than usual. Priscilla set the table and her mom put a pot of hot chicken soup on the table. Everyone came to the table when her mom said supper was ready. Priscilla noticed everyone looked tired but happy. The sun had been hot that day even though it was a beautiful day, and it had given some of them a slight red tint on their skin. Her mom and dad asked everyone how they liked their day today, and thanked them for being good. The table was filled with chatter and laughter, as they all put in their two cents about their day. Priscilla asked her mom when she would show her how to use the sewing machine. Her mom told her as soon as she herself was caught up with all of her sewing. Priscilla was content with that answer so she left it at that and gazed out the window at the pine trees. She loved watching their branches waving in the wind. She could smell the scent of pines coming in through the open windows. Sometimes it almost seemed like they were trying to tell her a story, and were softly whispering to her. She also loved the fresh smell of their scent. She leaned back to let her body relax and just breathed it in deeply and smiled to herself. Right now she was feeling extra greatful for their tightknit family that they had. -TO BE CONTINUED- (THE REST OF THE FOLLOWING IS POEMS I HAVE WRITTEN THAT I JUST WANTED ADDED TO THE BACK OF MY BOOK) (THE JOY OF PARENTS) The child was tiny and sweet and adorable as could be! With the perfect face and feet and toes adorable was she. They had never felt joy quite like this before. It was as if she had been washed in from the ocean shore! Their hearts were thrilled and filled with joy, and it did not matter to them that it was a girl instead of a boy. All wrapped up in a pink blanket so soft, it sure was not as if this happened as of oft! They vowed to raise their child and together they would stand, and if something bad happened they would just wave their magic wand! Sitting side by side, the parents sure were taking it in stride! Going home they were so they could put her in her brand new room, were there would surely never be any doom! She cooed and wiggled and moved her tiny feet and opened her eyes, and her parents she was so happy to meet! With everything done and put in its place, none other than she could give this room such grace! Love sure was the key, for who else could make it happen more than she! With everything so perfect and neat, off to bed they went and pulled up the sheets. Their mind and hearts were filled with such hope, and together they were confident they could cope! (CHILDREN AND THEIR DREAMS)Young as children they grow up with idea's big and small, and to grow up and make them happen they certainly want to do them all. School everyday they go until summer comes, oh how they can't wait to see what it has brung. They love playing at recess with their classmates, and a good lunch after they can't wait to taste! Sometimes the pressure of learning and writing their test's, can get their mind's in a frazzle and almost a mess. A break they have to have to refresh their head's, and help them to get good grades so they can sleep lightly when they go to bed! It's not always easy being a kid for learn they still have to do and grow up too, and not everything is always the way they want and the skies are not always blue. But parent's they have to fix their problems and bandage their wounds, oh how lucky they are that they have someone yet to catch them when they fall and blow up their balloons! How nice it is to have parent's to fix things when a kid, for it is not always easy to make the right bid. Birthday parties are thrown and fun is had, and at night cuddled up in their pajamas and tv they watch with their family until their eyes start closing just a tad. Dreams they dream in their soft beds, and hills with flowers and lollipops fill their little head's! In the morning wake up they do all new and refreshed, and brush their teeth they do to have minty breath. Hurry up they do to get ready for school, and a good breakfast they had so they can use their brain as a tool! Weekends they love to sleep in and then spend all day playing with their friends, and try they do so that the fun never ends! This is the life of happy children growing up, and remember their childhood they surely will and hopefully they will look back and see it as the half full cup!! (THE BOY WITH TATTERED SHOES) There was this boy who went to school you see. His shoes and shirt were as tattered as could be. Everyday he walked the mile and a half to school, with nary a lunchbox and a sandwich, but he thought it was cool. He did'nt need much to make him happy, for he thought he had the best ever ma and pappy! Every afternoon he came home he did his chores,and he sure did not have any time to be bored! He would fill the woodbox and then feed the chickens out behind the barn, yes he really did not mind helping out on the farm. He also had to bring in the cow from the field, and put her in the barn for her from the sun to shield. Maybe his clothes and shoes were tattered, but his love of his family was all that really mattered! When potatoes and meat got scarce they would look for wild food and plants, and then at night they would light their sturdy lamp. See kids can be happy, for all they need is a good ma and pappy! (RAKING LEAVES AT OUR HOME!!) Me and my brothers and sisters love this time of fall! We have had this tradition of raking leaves since we were small. We get all our rakes and join in the fun, giggling and laughing about we will run. We make the biggest pile ever, then take turns jumping in it like this idea was clever. We take turns covering each other up with leaves, oh how happy are times like these! The wind is always blowing this time of the year, and we are all attired in our fall gear. We like the myth of catching a leaf falling from a tree, for we get to make a wish for free. Wishes do come true, for everyone is special even you! But if true it does not come, there is certainly no time to be blue! For as many leaves as there are on a tree, that's how many wishes you can make for free! Chasing each other through the pile of leaves, sure does make us feel young and carefree. It is times like this when you realize, that you you don't even have to make a wish, for surely what could be better than this!? We are free as the leaves and fast as the wind and together we sure know how to have a merry time, and after all this fun it will surely take us awhile to unwind! How happy and peaceful are times like this, if only we could always stay in this state of bliss! The trees here sure do have a beauty all their own, and that is why we are so happy to call this our home!(FARING IN THE HILLS) I was young and free, and running in the hills with a spirit so free.The apple trees were starting to bloom with flowers so white, and it certainly did look like a heavenly sight.The grass was so fresh and green, and it was such a bright and beautiful scene! The air was warm and the sun was shining its bright rays. The smell of the flowers of the honeysuckles made me feel a special way. I really felt like my legs could sprint really fast. Days like this were such a blast! My spirit when in a place like this soared up high, just like the birds flying high in the sky. The freshness of the air penetrated my brain, and from happiness I could no longer refrain. It was like it set my spirit free, and sad I could no longer be! My health was great and my body was still so young! The fresh blackberries I picked nearby sure tasted good on my tongue. To make this perfect all I needed was to make myself a little teepee, and a fire to cook some nice hot tea! Oh yes that would make it perfect, and I would sit by the fire at night, so all the mosquito's would flee. Why with all this food growing in the wild,I could fare for myself even though I was still a child. With a summer like this, I could not even start to describe this feeling of bliss. See anybody with a will to live could do that here, with nary a soul to help them as many would fear. Yes I might still be a child, but what I can do for myself is not in the least mild. How satisfying it is to know, that if something ever happened I sure would know where to go! (I LOVE MY SISTERS) I love my sisters dear, for together we have nothing to fear. We are so much alike, and I think that is why sometimes we start a fight. But we both know the other always loves us, so that makes it all alright. When I am down I will call her, for there is nothing that will make me feel better then a sisterly "Get Together". We both come from the same father and mother, so I think that is why we are so much like one another. There is just something about family genes, that makes life so much easier when in need. Sisters understand each other for after all we have the same mother. We love to get together, and read each others love letters. Chatting over a nice cup of tea, is really very nice indeed! We like to talk about growing up and our childhood, and sometimes we would even like to go back for a bit if we could. But since it does not work that way, together as long as we can we will stay! Nobody understands each other like sisters, and how we like to search each others albums for some great pictures! I sure do love our sister bond, and of them I am so very fond! Together we are as often as we can, until we have to go home to our own man. We chat giggle and laugh, oh how sisters sure do make life go fast! Looking back at all our times we had together, I don't feel like it could be better! (A BOYS HAPPINESS OF A GOOD HOME) He fed the chickens and gathered the eggs out behind the barn, then went in the house were his mother was knitting with a roll of yarn. It was just getting dusk this time of night, and oh how everything about this felt just right! He loved his mother and father so dear, how glad was he they always were so near! His dad was still outside milking their cow, and he would be coming in anytime as of now. Supper was waiting on the table, and on it was their favorite sweetener maple! After supper was done and the dishes were put away, he went out and got their family dog so he would not go astray. After reading his favorite book, he went over to the pantry and a cookie he snook. It was his bedtime now, and outside the window grazing in the field chewing her cud was their cow. He took off his pants and shoes, and just then he heard the cow moo. As he jumped into bed he could hear the pitterpatter of rain on the roof, and the next thing he heard was the dog giving a woof! He could not feel any more satisfied and happy, for he sure liked his ma and pappy! (THE GOOD HUSBAND) The sun shone so nice and bright, as he picked up his hoe so light. The kids were playing so happy and carefree, as they happily gathered leaves for some good hot tea! The garden was so lush and green, and he was reminiscing when he was so young and lean. How he loved his seven kids and wife, and to him they were his life! The kids they taught how to make a good sustaining life, so that they could manage if they too sometime became man and wife. He worked very long and hard, for who else was to pay for the bread that required lard? His wife and kids would gather food in the fall, for when canned who would help eat it but all?! He loved the sound of his kids laughter, for when they were all tall and grown he would remember that after. You only live once in life, and if you miss that chance you will surely look back in strife. So to do it right once and for all, was his mission as sure as came fall. As he laid beside his wife in bed that night, he made sure he turned off the light. He felt as happy as could be, for the best ever wife was she! The kids were all tucked in bed nice and tight, and he knew they would all be up at the crack of light. He hugged his wife so nice and sweet, oh how happy he was that they could meet!

This book is written about a young girl who grew up in a pioneer way of living and loves to try out her adventurous skills and loves her family. She likes to dream and has many ideas about her future ahead. Her family never had electricity, indoors bathroom, or running water and lived the life of the old timers. I promise you one thing.... and that is you will not be bored reading this book!

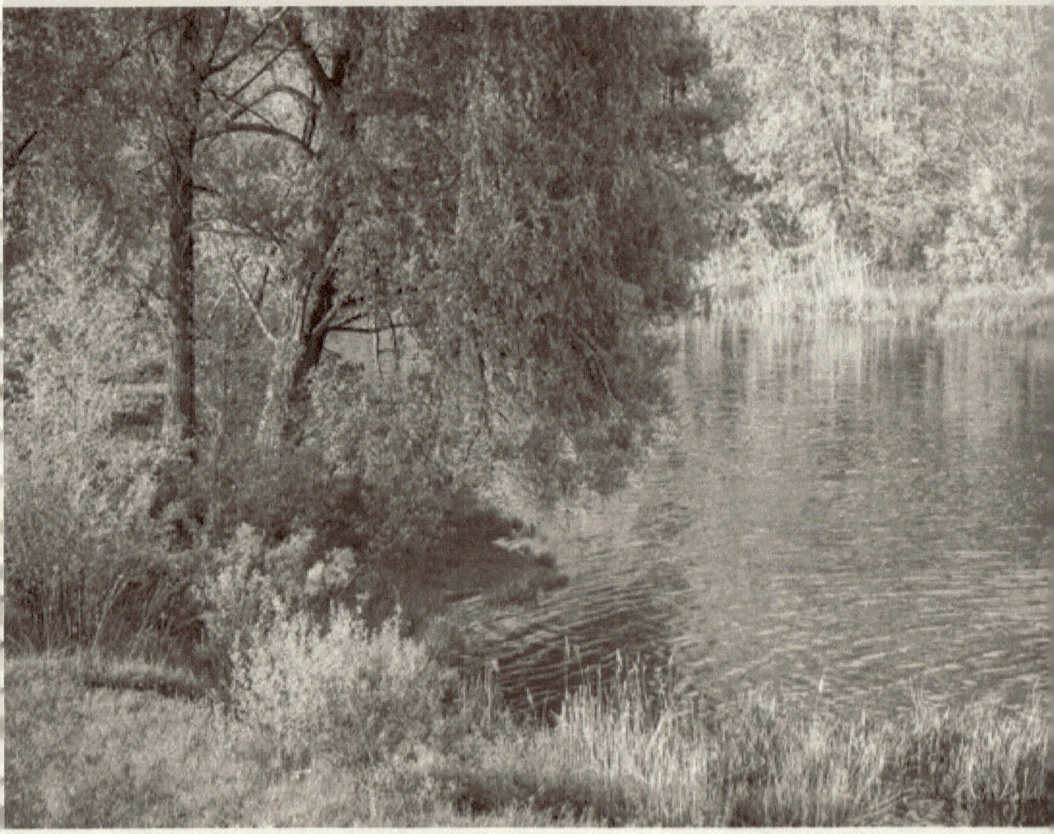

Hi, I love to write and inspire other readers and encourage children to look forward to every day and dream about exciting new adventures

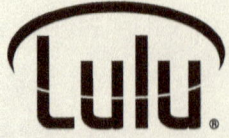